Rob Gronkowski

A Biography of the Hard-Hitting Superstar

BENJAMIN SOUTHERLAND

Visit Benjamin Southerland's website at
benjaminsoutherland.com.

ISBN-13: 978-1521212240

Table of Contents

Chapter 1: Superstar in Gordy's Fitness Shop

Rob Gronkowski grew up in what many would consider a mad house. Rob's father, Gordy, had five sons who were all very active in sports. Gordy tried to get recruited to play either college baseball or football, and one day, on a visit, the football coach at Syracuse saw Gordy taking batting practice, and the next thing you know, Gordy was playing defensive end. He was often injured and moved around between defense and offensive line but had a decent college career. He made it to training camp at the United States Football League, a short-lived challenger to the NFL, and was offered a job with the Canadian Football League. Staying in football at that level proved unaffordable, however, and Gordy quit the game to go to work in sales for an oil company called Superior outside Buffalo, New York.

Gordy had five sons: Gordie Jr., born in 1983; Dan, born in 1985; Chris, born in 1986; Rob, born in 1989; and

Glenn, born in 1990. In the midst of all that, Gordy was inspired to try opening a fitness store. He founded G&G Fitness with his brother in 1990. It was a side business at first, but after a few years, working two jobs became overwhelming and Gordy had to step back from his day job at Superior. By the time the boys were getting into sports, their dad was working full time in the equipment business and the boys had access to all the equipment and fitness knowledge they could possibly need. Their mom, Diane, ensured proper nutrition, and when the boys got to high school, Gordy set them up with professional strength training. Gordie Jr. would go on to play minor league baseball while Dan, Chris, and Glenn would play in the NFL, Dan as a tight end and Chris and Glenn as fullbacks. All are impressive athletes in their own right, but so far Rob has been the superstar of the family.

The family all remember the boys being incredibly competitive with each other growing up. Having five boys so close together in age meant they could play a variety of games, like two-on-two basketball or roller hockey. Rob was very popular, but he was not a perfect kid. He would occasionally get into fights, and he once crashed while recklessly racing a four-wheeler and injured his knee fairly seriously. He hid the injury from his parents until it turned out he had a serious infection caused by a piece of wood shrapnel stuck under his skin. He also once broke a backboard during warm-ups at a rival team's basketball court and was accused of doing that on purpose.

The Gronkowski boys were not allowed to play organized football until the eighth grade, as Gordy worried about their safety. By high school, though, Rob was playing basketball, football, and baseball. He played on the varsity basketball team his freshman year, which was unheard of. Rob's high school coach believes Rob could have played college basketball at the highest levels, but Rob was focused on football. He was called up to the varsity football team late in his freshman year and played receiver and defensive end. When Rob's senior year rolled around, Gordy was supervising the construction of a new store in Pittsburgh, and Rob was getting into some trouble in New York. So Rob moved to Pittsburgh to live with his dad.

Coincidentally or not, Pittsburgh also had a much higher level of football, and the move created some controversy among those who follow high school sports. It even got some national press. Star players are not supposed to move around to try and find a better place to play. Regardless of the motives for the move, the higher level of competition and greater visibility helped Rob develop more complete skills. For example, he was called on to block in the running game for his new team instead of simply going out to catch passes against inferior competition on every play like he did in Buffalo. Rob would later say that the year in Pittsburgh was almost like a freshman year of college, where he had to step into a completely new situation with a much higher level of competition. The increased visibility also helped with Rob's college recruiting. He was heavily recruited, but he had visited the University of Arizona already while his brother Chris was being recruited, and Rob pretty much decided that was the right place for him. Arizona was the first school to offer Rob a spot on their team, and he took it.

Chapter 2: Flashes as a Wildcat and a Bad Back

In his book, *It's Good to be Gronk*, he describes being a bit shell shocked by his first practice with the Arizona Wildcats. He said he worked hard, and of his physique stated, "I was huge at 270 pounds, I had no excess weight and my six-pack was tight." He reveled in the opportunity to stonewall pass rushers, but it was not easy at first. Once he mastered that, he had to learn to run routes with defenders aggressively jamming him at the line of scrimmage. This was not a skill he had developed in high school. He got himself ready though and had the rare opportunity to start as a true freshman in the team's first game, against Brigham Young University. He caught one pass for 17 yards, and even though his team lost, he later said that getting rid of those "first-catch jitters" was a crucial step in his development. The next week he picked up 65 yards and a touchdown in a win against Northern Arizona.

Arizona lost its next two games and Rob played poorly. He felt like he was struggling to get open, which was not really necessary when he was in high school. He kept working at it, and sure enough, things fell in place in the fifth game of the season, against Washington State. Arizona won big, powered by 115 yards and two touchdowns from Gronk. He described the rest of the season as a roller coaster. He would swing from no catches against Oregon State to six catches for 94 yards and a touchdown against UCLA. He finished the season with 28 catches for 525 yards. It was a very solid season for a freshman, setting a school record for receiving yards by a tight end and earning All-American honors. The team was nothing special, though, and finished the season with a losing record of six wins and seven losses. Gronk wasted no time enjoying his offseason with parties in "Club G," an off-campus apartment he rented with his brother Gordie Jr., who had recently graduated from college.

Gronk trained hard all offseason at home with retired NFL player Demeris Johnson, and his brother Chris Gronkowski also joined him on the Arizona team that year. Unfortunately, Rob came down with mono at the beginning of the 2008 season and had to miss the first three games; the first two were blowout wins, against lesser opponents Idaho and Toledo, and the third was a loss to New Mexico. His first game back was against rival UCLA, and he caught two touchdowns to get the Wildcats back on track. He followed that up with a monster performance against Washington, catching five balls for 109 yards and three touchdowns. From there out, it seemed like Arizona could not be stopped when Gronk was having a good game. He was quiet in a loss to Stanford. He put up 104 yards and a touchdown in a win against the University of California and then 83 yards and a touchdown in a win over Washington State. Arizona narrowly lost to both Oregon and Oregon State, but Rob did keep up his production in those games, putting up 193 yards and two touchdowns combined. Both Chris and Rob put up decent numbers in the finale against Brigham Young University, with Rob putting up four catches and 27 yards, while Chris had two catches for 43 yards and a touchdown. Rob finished the season with 47 catches for 672 yards and 10 touchdowns.

Rob was very excited for his junior year. NFL scouts were starting to view him as a first- or second-round draft pick, and his dad was able to negotiate an insurance policy to protect against injury. Gordy signed a deal that said if Rob was unable to play more than a couple games in the NFL, Rob could walk away from football and pocket $4 million tax free. That wound up being a hard choice. While lifting weights in the offseason, Rob ruptured a disc in his back. He ignored the injury until it began to slow him down to the point where he felt no strength in his legs. He tried rehab to get back onto the field for the Wildcats, but finally he decided to shut himself down for the season and undergo back surgery.

During rehab from the back surgery, Rob had a choice to make. He could (1) return to Arizona for his senior year, (2) quit football and take his $4 million, or (3) declare for the NFL draft. He had the option to try to make it in the NFL but quit and take his insurance money after a couple games, and that was appealing. He rehabbed and trained for the NFL Combine with Pete Bommarito in Miami, Florida, and hired heavy-hitter Drew Rosenhaus to be his agent. Ultimately, his rehab was going well but he could not risk another season of college, so he declared himself eligible for the NFL draft.

Most top draft picks attend the NFL Combine to perform a series of drills for scouts and also have meetings and medical evaluations with NFL teams. Gronk did things a little bit differently. He attended the NFL Combine to meet with teams, but he did not work out. His private training told him he was not prepared to put forth a respectable effort. He continued to rehab and worked out later at the Arizona pro day, running a 4.63 40-yard dash and registering a vertical of 33.5 inches, both impressive for a tight end. During this recruiting process he had positive meetings with the Baltimore Ravens, Denver Broncos, Miami Dolphins, and New England Patriots, but after night one and the first round of the draft, none of these teams had taken him. He had to wait until the second round, which was a bit of a let down given his production in his junior year of college, but he was confident he would get picked early in the second round the next day. Rumor had it he was on track to get picked by the Baltimore Ravens at number 43 overall. As he was getting ready for that pick, however, the Patriots swooped in with a trade and picked Gronk with the 42nd pick.

Chapter 3: Setting the NFL on Fire

The Patriots are known for their no-nonsense attitude and Gronk was known for his silliness, so the two were an interesting pair. The Pats were led by Bill Belichick, whose dour personality and reclusive nature set the tone for the team's public relations. Belichick won two Super Bowls as the defensive coordinator for the New York Giants, and he brought that defensive mentality to the Patriots. He combined a dominant defense with reliable quarterback play from an unheralded young quarterback named Tom Brady to win Super Bowl championships in 2001, 2003, and 2004.

After 2004, the Patriots moved on from many of their key defensive players and the unit became less dominant. At the same time, Brady developed into one of the best quarterbacks in the league. In 2007, the Patriots pulled receivers Wes Welker and Randy Moss into their stable of pass catchers. These two would form a dominant tandem, with Welker reliably picking up short yardage and Moss stretching the defense with his ability to pull in deep balls. In 2007, the Patriots went undefeated in the regular season and broke all kinds of scoring records, only to lose a heartbreaker in the Super Bowl against the New York Giants. Welker and Moss would continue to lead the passing game in 2008 with backup quarterback Matt Cassel playing for an injured Tom Brady, and then with Brady again in 2009. Their production over these three seasons is among the best for any pair of receivers in NFL history, but by 2010 Welker and Moss were starting to get into their mid-30s and the pair could not be around forever.

Gronkowski was widely considered a good draft pick, but his selection was not major news. Blogger Greg Knopping gave the pick a solid thumbs up, saying Gronk was a "Great all around TE with great hands, great size." He called Gronk a steal in the second round and said Gronk was in the driver's seat for the starting tight end job. Overall, though, Rob Gronkowski mostly earned a shrug. Writer Ryan Lester, for example, said Gronk and the other New England tight ends had little to offer from a fantasy perspective.

Much more commentary was given to the other tight end that the Patriots drafted that year, Aaron Hernandez of the University of Florida Gators. Writers like the *Boston Globe*'s Albert Breer said that Hernandez was perhaps the "most dangerous" pass-catching tight end in the draft and a possible first-round talent, but he had a history of failed drug tests at Florida and that prompted many teams to take him off their boards. Patriots' Coach Bill Belichick is friendly with Florida's Coach Urban Meyer, and Hernandez reportedly told teams the marijuana was used to help him cope with the death of his father. That was apparently enough to ease Belichick's fears, and the Patriots took Hernandez in the fourth round.

Together, the Gronk and Hernandez picks were seen as a potentially large shift for the Patriots. Rich Hill noted that the Patriots had a poor history of offensive production at the tight end position. The team had drafted many, including Georgia standout Benjamin Watson in the first round in 2004. Hill argued that perhaps the Patriots were moving on from trying to find an all-around great tight end and instead trying to create a dynamic pair with the run-blocking Rob Gronkowski and the pure pass-catcher Aaron Hernandez. This analysis downplayed Gronk's pass-catching skills.

The Gronk-Hernandez pairing put the Pats on the leading edge of the rise of the pass-catching tight end. Tight ends were traditionally linemen who blocked in the run game, and it would be a nice bonus if they were also able to catch a few passes when a play broke down. In recent years, tight ends have come into the league in a wider variety of roles. Some, like Jimmy Graham, could almost be considered big wide receivers with marginal blocking skills. Hernandez fit into that mold. Gronkowski was something special, however, because he had great run-blocking skills paired with playmaking abilities in the passing game. That meant that when he is in the game, defenses cannot be sure if he is going to block or run a receiving route. Having both players allowed the Patriots to run a variety of formations and wreak havoc on defenses.

The 2010 offseason had some speed bumps. Tom Brady and Randy Moss were both dealing with contract negotiations. Brady eventually got a deal and Moss did not. This seems to have led to some bad blood. Tom Brady also smashed up his car in a crash in early September. He walked away but gave the team a scare. Through all that, Gronk and Hernandez seemed to integrate well into their new surroundings, but the two new tight ends did not draw a ton of attention as the season was getting started.

Rob hit the NFL turf for the first time on September 19, 2010, in a preseason game against the Atlanta Falcons, and the two-tight-end tandem was off and running. Gronk caught four passes for a total of 38 yards, and that included a highlight-reel grab in tight coverage for a 24-yard touchdown from backup quarterback Brian Hoyer. Hernandez added four catches for 46 yards and a touchdown of his own. Gronk would be the story for the rest of the preseason. The next week, the Patriots played the St. Louis Rams, and Gronk put up 66 yards and three touchdowns. Rob scored the first touchdown while dragging a defender that was hanging onto his leg, and that image was certainly burned into the minds of smaller cornerbacks around the league. Rob closed out his preseason by catching another touchdown against the New York Giants.

The Patriots' first regular-season game, against the Cincinnati Bengals, showed the Gronk-Hernandez potential, but it also showed the Patriots had a logjam among pass catchers and there may not be enough balls to go around. Both tight ends had big catches, Hernandez for 45 yards and Gronkowski for a one-yard touchdown. That was it, though. Wes Welker had eight catches and two touchdowns; Randy Moss had five; and both Ben Tate and Kevin Faulk had four. He was fighting for targets, but Gronk could not help but be excited. After the game he said, "It was a great feeling to get the first touchdown…Going out there, your heart's pounding when I was first out there. Last night, too. A lot of nerves, but after the first couple of drives, it gets out of you. It's like playing football again."

The two tight ends slowly took over a leading role in the offense. Week two was all Hernandez, as he caught six passes for 101 yards to lead all receivers, and Gronk chipped in one catch for 14 yards in a loss to the New

York Jets. The next week, it was Hernandez on top again with six catches for 65 yards and Gronk with three catches for 43 yards and a touchdown. The Patriots won their fourth game of the season, against the Miami Dolphins, in a blowout, but something seemed wrong with the passing game. The pass-happy Patriots scored touchdowns on a returned interception, a blocked field goal attempt, a kickoff return, and two runs from running backs. Gronk and Hernandez combined for only 33 yards. Rumors began to circulate that Randy Moss, who was in the last year of his contract, was frustrated and wanted to either get paid or get out of town.

The next week it was confirmed that there was trouble in paradise when Randy Moss was traded to the Minnesota Vikings for a third-round pick. It was a bit of a shock, as Brady had just told the press that "Randy is important, was important, and will be important" to the team. Reports later surfaced that Moss asked for a trade after feeling "unwanted" because of his contract status and declining number of targets, and that appeared to be true. The Patriots made a second move to help compensate for the loss, bringing back former Patriot and friend of Brady's Deion Branch in a trade. Coach Belichick said he was confident in the pass catchers he had left on the team, and that turned out to be a good call.

In the next game, against the Baltimore Ravens, Hernandez and Branch would lead the passing game, but

Rob had a key 24-yard catch late in the fourth quarter to force overtime, where the Pats would go on to win. It was the same story the next week in a nail-biter of a win against the San Diego Chargers, with Hernandez and Branch leading the way for the passing game but Gronkowski collecting a key touchdown. Both Gronk and Hernandez were quiet in a win over the Minnesota Vikings the next week, with just three catches between them.

By week nine, it was clear that the rookie tight ends were the focal point of the offense. Aaron Hernandez had five catches for 48 yards and two touchdowns, while Gronkowski had four for 47 in a loss to the Browns, but the Pats rebounded against the Pittsburgh Steelers with Gronkowski making five catches for 72 yards and three very impressive touchdowns. Over the next seven games, Gronkowski would go on to make at least one catch in each of the last seven games, for a total of 23 catches for 326 yards and four touchdowns. Hernandez would miss time because of an injury, but would add 11 catches for 127 yards. Gronkowski's 10 touchdown catches for the season were a franchise record for a rookie. He pulled in 42 total catches for 546 yards. The team played well, also. They finished the season with a league-best 14-2 record and were heavily favored against their rival Jets in their first playoff game.

Rob's first trip to the postseason did not go well, though. The lead up to the game was a bit strange. The Jets were coached by the notoriously brash Rex Ryan, and his players taunted the notoriously buttoned-up Patriots. Jets cornerback Antonio Cromartie, for example, called Tom Brady an "a--hole," and Brady responded that Cromartie was a "good player." More strangely, photos purportedly of Rex Ryan and his wife engaged in some kind of foot-focused sexual activity were leaked onto the Internet. Wes Welker decided to make a joke of the whole situation, "putting his best foot forward" by working 11 references to feet into his press conference before the game.

The Patriots may have been feeling cocky after defeating the Jets 43 to 3 in the regular season, but that turned out to be a mistake. In hindsight, it was easy to see that the Jets were a serious threat. They had a strong secondary led by all-world defensive back Darrelle Revis, and the Patriots' defense had been incredibly leaky all season. Coach Belichick added a degree of difficulty when he benched Wes Welker to start the game, presumably a punishment for the foot jokes (he would never say). The Jets jammed the Patriots receivers at the line, throwing off their timing. On one fateful third down, this jamming knocked Gronk off balance and he dropped a short pass. The Patriots botched a fake punt on the next play, and things spiraled downhill from there. Rob finished with four receptions for 67 yards, but the Patriots lost in what is still considered perhaps the worst playoff failure in franchise history.

The season certainly had come to a disappointing close, but it was hard for the Pats to not be excited about the future. The team had moved on from Randy Moss and stayed one of the top offenses in the league. The defense had issues, but the team was young on both sides of the ball and was set up for a large draft class the next year owing to past trades. Commentators like Jeff Howe were expecting a big year with Gronk and Hernandez exceeding their combined 87 catches, 1,109 yards, and 16 touchdowns, as they were to become more comfortable with the offense and in sync with Brady. Gronk told his family he expected a big year, joking he could get 20 touchdowns. It turns out they were not thinking big enough.

The Patriots put a major focus on the offense in the 2011 draft. They picked up tackles Nate Solder in the first round and Marcus Cannon in the fifth round. They also grabbed running backs Shane Vereen and Stevan Ridley in the second and third rounds. All four players would go on to be significant contributors for the team. The team picked up another tight end, Lee Smith, in the fifth round, but Smith never caught on.

Gronk sat out the preseason, presumably just as a precaution, and then he joined the Patriots to come out roaring against the Miami Dolphins in their first game of the 2011 season. Brady threw for a career-high 517 yards and four touchdowns. Hernandez picked up 103 yards and a touchdown, while Gronk had 86 and a touchdown of his own. This marked somewhat of a turning point where the football world began to really pay attention to the Gronk and Hernandez machine. They were beginning to look comfortable and Brady was showing faith in them. Brady, Gronk, Hernandez, and the Pats became an unstoppable freight train.

The next week in a win against the San Diego Chargers, it was Gronk in the lead with four catches, 86 yards, and two touchdowns while Hernandez chipped in seven catches, 62 yards, and one touchdown. Hernandez was injured in that game and Gronk increased his load in the ensuing games. Back in his hometown of Buffalo, Gronk had another big night with two touchdowns and 109 yards, though the Patriots suffered an upset loss. The train rolled on. He logged 15, 31, and 74 yards respectively in wins against the Raiders, Jets, and Cowboys. Rob got himself into a little bit of trouble over the bye week that year, as he went back home to hang out with a group of friends. He snapped a fateful picture with a friend of a friend, an adult actress named Bibi Jones. She posted some pictures online of them together and it became a bit of a sensation. They both insist nothing happened between them, but the Patriots did not seem overly impressed with his choice of company. Back on the field, the Patriots hit a bit of a rough patch with close losses back to back against Pittsburgh and the New York Giants. Gronk did his part, though, logging 195 yards and a touchdown in the two games combined.

The rest of the regular season was pure fire for both the Patriots and Rob Gronkowski. The team won every game and Gronkowski scored a touchdown in most of them. By midseason, Greg Bedard of the *Boston Globe* said, "Gronkowski is on a course to become the greatest tight end in NFL history." In just the 12th game of the season, a big win against Indianapolis, he briefly broke the NFL record for receiving touchdowns by a tight end in a year with 14. Unfortunately, after the game, one of his touchdowns was ruled a lateral and therefore a rushing touchdown. He had no need to worry. The next game he caught six passes for 160 yards and two touchdowns, and the record was secured. He would wrap up the regular season with a big game against Buffalo, 108 yards and two touchdowns. He finished the regular season with 90 catches for an NFL record 1,327 yards and 17 touchdowns, plus that one rushing touchdown. The Patriots finished with a 13 to 3 record and went into another postseason with great expectations.

The first playoff game was at home against the Denver Broncos, who that year were riding the magic carpet ride known as Tebowmania. Tim Tebow had just pulled off a string of improbable victories to get his team into the postseason, and then the Broncos defeated the Steelers in an overtime, upset victory. It was one of the greatest stories in sports, but the Patriots methodically ended Tebow's magic ride (and, it would turn out, his NFL career) with a 45 to 10 victory. Tom Brady threw six touchdowns, including three to Gronkowski and one to Hernandez. Gronk would finish the game with 10 catches for 45 yards, including one catch that Brady called "one of the best catches I've ever seen." The game was also the first playoff win for the Pats since 2007.

Next up was the AFC Championship Game against the Baltimore Ravens. This game is a great but tragic moment in Patriots lore for a number of reasons. First, Tom Brady played very poorly, throwing two interceptions and no touchdowns. Gronk and Hernandez led all receivers, with a total of five catches and 87 yards for Gronk and seven catches for 66 yards for Hernandez. It was a moment where the tight ends carried their struggling quarterback. But then Gronk took a blow to the knee in the third quarter and had to leave the game temporarily. The hit was delivered by Bernard Pollard, the "Patriot Killer" who tore Tom Brady's ACL in 2008 and Wes Welker's in 2010.

The Patriots managed to scrape together a 23 to 20 lead at the end of the game, but the Ravens were driving. The Patriots defense was pretty beat up, to the point where wide receiver Julian Edelman was playing safety. Ravens quarterback Joe Flacco put a beauty of a pass right into the breadbasket of receiver Lee Evans, but at the last minute Patriots defender Sterling Moore knocked the ball loose. The Ravens then settled for a field goal to send the game to overtime, but kicker Billy Cundiff missed one of the all-time heartbreakers from just 32 yards out. He blamed some confusion on the scoreboard for rushing his kick, and there have been some conspiracy theories that the Patriots fooled with the scoreboard to make the kick harder. The Patriots were left feeling more lucky than good, but happy to move on to the Super Bowl. The game was also memorable for Rob coining one of his most famous catchphrases when a reporter from ESPN Deportes asked him if he was going to celebrate and he said, "Si. Yo soy fiesta" (Translated: "Yes. I am party").

The victory led to a Super Bowl rematch between the Patriots and the New York Giants, who had spoiled the Patriots' perfect season in 2007. Rob Gronkowski dominated headlines leading into the matchup. First, there was the injury. He missed practice and was spotted in an ankle boot, and he admitted to reporters his status was uncertain. He said, "the game is six days away, I can be 100 percent by then or I can be 2 percent by then."

Reporters also focused on his unique skills and how he was changing the game, which included marveling over his huge hands and success at catching the ball. Gronk's rise in popular culture was also apparent, as rapper Timbaland wrote a song about the superstar. The Patriots were 12-point favorites going into the game, and were widely expected to avenge their 2007 loss. Belichick was awarded the Coach of the Year award coming into the game, just to top things off.

The game got off to a rough start for New England, though. The Giants got the ball first, and after their drive stalled out, they downed their first punt at the Patriots six-yard line. Brady threw his first pass from his own end zone and launched the ball deep to nobody. He was called for intentional grounding, and just like that, the Pats were down 2 to 0 and on the defensive again. The Giants methodically moved the ball down the field, and quarterback Eli Manning capped off the drive with a touchdown to wide receiver Victor Cruz, a fellow rising star in the NFL who then broke out his signature salsa dance celebration.

The next drive for the Pats was a little better. Brady hit his favorite wideouts Deion Branch and Wes Welker for big gains, and the Patriots scored a field goal. By this time, it was starting to become clear that Gronk was not quite right. The two teams traded punts back and forth for a while until the last drive of the half. Brady got that drive moving with a big pass to Gronk for 20 yards. Gronk could not get much separation but was able to turn around and snag the ball out of the air in traffic. Brady then added passes of 10 and 8 yards to Hernandez. A couple quick hits for running back Danny Woodhead right before the half, and the Pats scored a touchdown and headed to the locker room up 10 to 9.

In the second half, it looked like the Pats might put things away. They moved down the field quickly, and Brady hit Hernandez for a touchdown to put the Patriots up 17 to 9. From there, the Giants just kept chipping away. The Giants scored a field goal; the Patriots went three and out; and then the Giants scored another field goal. It was now 17 to 15. Early in the fourth quarter, the Patriots were putting a drive together and Brady reared back and launched one deep down the field to Gronk, but he could not get there and the ball was picked off. The clock continued to wind down without any more scoring. The Pats had a chance to end the game up 17 to 15 with just one more first down, but Wes Welker failed to pull in a tough catch and the Patriots had to punt. Eli Manning put together a magical drive to put the Giants up 21 to 17 with just 57 seconds left. The Pats moved the ball a little, but the clock ran out on another season. Rob Gronkowski was in place for a Hail Mary at the end of the game, but he could not bring it in and finished the biggest game of his life with just two catches for 26 yards.

Chapter 4: Struggles, Injury and Otherwise

Up to this point, Rob Gronkowski had lived a charmed NFL life. He had started in all 32 regular-season games plus four playoff games of his career, making at least one catch in each. Sure, he twisted up his ankle and had a subpar Super Bowl, but just making it that far was an accomplishment and he was breaking records left and right. The injury was unfortunate but did not seem to be serious. But Super Bowl losing teams have a bit of a curse, and the Patriots did not seem immune. Plus, Gronk would say he was haunted by the missed Hail Mary and interception he could not pull in during the Super Bowl.

Gronk had his first real taste of controversy when he was spotted partying like a wild man on his bad ankle at a LMFAO concert just after the Super Bowl. In his book, he called the criticism by fans unfair, but said, "if it pissed you off, it might make you feel better to know I woke up the next morning with a heck of a hangover."

Many observers also began to wonder if the game had been the last chance for Brady, because the team would have to replace him soon. Overall, though, the Patriots seemed to be on the upswing. Gronk and Hernandez were only 22 years old and had combined for 2,237 yards and 24 touchdowns in the 2011 season, making them by far the most productive duo in the NFL. Gronk's surgery was reportedly successful, and the injury was not considered a long-term problem. Plus, the Patriots then loaded up on defense in the draft.

By his own telling, Gronk had a great summer. He partied, rehabbed, and traveled with his brothers. He also negotiated a contract extension with the Patriots, worth $54 million over six years. It was the biggest contract ever for a tight end at the time, but the 2012 season would be the end of the charmed football life for Rob Gronkowski.

Gronk would again roll through the early part of the season, but the injuries started to creep up. Meanwhile, Hernandez was missing time with an ankle problem. Gronk would later admit his back started really bothering him after week two, but he still started the first 10 games and had at least two catches in each. His total numbers at the time were 53 catches for 746 yards and 10 touchdowns. The Patriots were putting together a solid record at 7 and 3. Disaster struck, though, while the Patriots were demolishing the Indianapolis Colts in week

10. Up 35 points late in the fourth quarter, Gronk was out doing his special teams duty of blocking for an extra point attempt, and he broke his forearm. The team, and Coach Belichick who has a reputation for running up the score, took some criticism for having their star blocking for a meaningless extra point.

Hernandez would come back while Gronk sat several weeks. Gronk would have surgery to screw his bones back together and come back for the final regular-season game, making two catches and scoring a touchdown against the Dolphins. His playoff run would be short, however. The Patriots' first playoff game was against the Houston Texans, and on the second drive, Gronk went streaking down the sideline and Brady threw it deep. Gronk could not haul it in and hit the ground pretty hard. It did not look like a serious fall, but Gronk was quickly ruled out for the game with a re-injured forearm. The Patriots would go on to win, powered by three touchdowns from Shane Vereen, but they would lose the next week without Gronk in a rematch of the previous year's Ravens vs. Patriots AFC Championship Game.

The 2013 offseason was awful. Rob would go on to have three more surgeries on his forearm. First, he had to fix up the second break of the bone. Then, he came down with a nasty staph infection and had to have a third surgery to take out the infected hardware in his arm and replace it. The bone still would not heal, so he had to have a bone graft where bone from his leg was turned into gel and put into his forearm. The repeat surgeries set his rehab back, so while he was out of commission, he went ahead and had another procedure to clear up the problem in his back. That was five surgeries over a span of a few months, following two seasons of excellent health. During this time, there were growing rumors that the Patriots and the Gronkowski family were not on the same page regarding his rehab and use. Some felt that Gronk was rushed back too fast to help the team in the short term and that was costing Gronk in the long term. In fact, the arm injury had reached the level where it could be career threatening.

Gronk's injury woes paled in comparison to the images splashed across TV screens from the Hernandez residence in June of that year. Aaron had been arrested for murdering a friend, a semi-pro football player who had been dating a relative of Hernandez's fiancée. Hernandez was instantly dropped from the team, and the Patriots expressed their condolences and then soon refused to talk to the media. Gronk would have his fair share of awkward moments, like when he almost walked out on an interview with CBS News that veered into the Hernandez story. The media was captivated by stories of the murder and discord between Gronk and the Patriots regarding his rehab.

The team needed Gronk back. At the beginning of 2011, Tom Brady had been throwing to Hall of Famer Randy Moss, possible Hall of Famer Wes Welker, and the best tight-end duo in the league. He started 2013 without any of them, as Welker had been awkwardly dropped in the offseason like Moss the year before, and Hernandez was in jail. That left Brady throwing to rookie receivers Aaron Dobson and Kenbrell Thompkins, both of whom struggled. Danny Amendola, who was brought in to replace Welker, was also struggling. Julian Edelman, who had been primarily a special teams player, was a silver lining as he began to mesh with Brady and take on a starring role. The lead up to each of the first six games centered on whether Gronk would play, and before each game, it was decided that he would not.

So the team was relieved when Gronk finally got back onto the field for game seven of the season. The Pats had been skating by on Tom Brady heroics and had somehow managed a five and one record, but that did not seem sustainable. Gronk was solid in his return, catching eight passes for 114 yards. He would later say he felt weak and slow, but he would get stronger. His best game of the season came in week three, when he caught nine passes for 143 yards and a touchdown in a blowout of the Pittsburgh Steelers. He caught a touchdown in each of the next three games, including an absolutely legendary comeback win in overtime against the Denver Broncos.

But in just his seventh game back, he went deep down the seam, and right as he caught the ball, Browns safety T.J. Ward flew headfirst into his knee. Gronk suffered a torn ACL and MCL, and would later find out he was also concussed. It was a brutal scene, and the game came to a standstill while medics carried him off the field and teammates and opponents came over to wish him well. The team would struggle without him, but finish the season a respectable 12 and 4. They crushed the Colts in the first round of the playoffs but could not manufacture any offense in the second half of an AFC Championship loss to the Denver Broncos.

Chapter 5: Don't Call It a Comeback—Super Bowl Champs

Gronk rehabbed hard all offseason, but many fans were apprehensive about the offense for the upcoming season. The Patriots failed to pick up any new pass-catching options in the draft, opting instead for an oft-injured defensive lineman in the first round and a new backup quarterback, Jimmy Garoppolo, in the second round. Free agency also came and went without any major help on offense. The defense was another story, with a number of injured players returning and the team also picking up Darrelle Revis, one of the league's top defensive backs. Overall, the Patriots were expected to have a good season and compete for a Super Bowl, but Gronk was going to have to perform.

Perceptions of the Patriots really dropped in the first four games. Gronk played every one but was used sparingly.

The first game was an upset loss to division rival Miami. Gronk scored a touchdown but had only 40 yards total. It was a similar story for Gronk the next two weeks, but the Patriots won. Then came the Kansas City Chiefs on *Monday Night Football*, a night that lives in infamy for Patriots fans. Tom Brady had a complete meltdown, including a pick thrown towards Gronk, and then got benched when the game was out of hand. Gronk continued to play and picked up a tough touchdown from backup quarterback Jimmy Garoppolo. That provided a little fuel for the next week.

The 14 to 44 blowout by the Chiefs on national TV was a tough loss for the Pats. TV analyst Trent Dilfer declared "They're just not good anymore," and a reporter asked Coach Belichick if he would be evaluating the quarterback position. Coach Belichick, Gronk, and the rest of the team stayed focused and insisted they were "on to Cincinnati," which was the next game on the schedule. Gronk also told friends he was going to make Brady look like himself again. Cincinnati was coming into the matchup undefeated, and the Patriots were struggling and had a short week, so the Patriots were the underdog.

The Pats silenced their critics for one night at least, as Gronk helped crush the Bengals in a 17 to 43 blowout. He led all receivers with six receptions for 100 yards and a touchdown. Afterwards, people began to say that it seemed like the old Gronk was back. Gronk felt it too. He said after the game, he was back to being fearless and ready to dominate. Gronk put up solid games of 94 and 68 yards in wins against the Bills and Jets respectively, and then he delivered one of his most dominant games ever against the Chicago Bears. Gronk scored early and then came back for more. He caught a ball about 15 yards deep and was grabbed almost immediately by a defender, but Gronk threw him down like a rag doll and kept trucking all the way to the end zone for a 46-yard touchdown. He would finish with three touchdowns and 149 yards in a 51 to 23 win.

As the season wore on, Gronk got stronger and so did the New England defense. Gronk was back to being a model of consistency, catching at least three balls every game and putting up big yardage numbers. The only major hiccup for the Pats or Gronk came in Green Bay, when the Pats lost and Gronk dropped a potentially game-winning pass in the final moments of the game. He sat out the last game of the season as the Patriots had their playoff seeding set, but finished with 82 catches, 1,124 yards, and 12 touchdowns. It was remarkable production given that he was now a focal point for opposing defenses. More importantly, he started off the postseason healthy.

First up was another playoff rematch with the Baltimore Ravens. The Patriots' run game struggled and the Ravens were putting up points, so it was up to Tom Brady and his pass catchers to win the game. In their last possession before halftime, the Patriots were trailing 14 to 0, but Gronk got the offense moving by hauling in a deep 46-yard pass. Gronk's next catch helped drive the Patriots to their second touchdown, and that catch also helped Brady set a new all-time career postseason passing yards record. Brady later made a huge mistake trying to get the ball to Gronk deep late in the second quarter and instead threw an interception, leading to another Ravens touchdown and setting the halftime score at Baltimore 21 New England 14. The Ravens would score to start the second half, and now it was 28 to 14 and the Patriots had to dig deep.

The Patriots' comeback started with some trickery from another tight end, Michael Hoomanawanui or Hoo Man. Running back Shane Vereen lined up on the right side of the formation and acted like he was going out for a pass, but he had actually declared himself ineligible. That automatically made Hoo Man an eligible receiver, but to the defense, it looked like Hoo Man was a blocker so they did not guard him. Brady hit Hoo Man twice in rapid succession, picking up 16 then 10 yards, plus an extra five yards when Baltimore coach John Harbaugh delayed the game to protest the Patriots' play. The move was deemed legal (though the NFL would later make it illegal) and Brady capped off the drive with a short touchdown pass to Gronk. That helped Brady tie the all-time playoff record for touchdown passes. Brady broke that record with one more touchdown pass, and then the New England defense was able to hang on for a thrilling 35 to 31 victory.

Gronk was fairly quiet in the next game, which will forever live in infamy in the history of the NFL. Running back LeGarrette Blount would do most of the work, notching 148 yards and three touchdowns. Gronk chipped in 28 yards and a touchdown, and tackle Nate Solder and fullback James Develin also got in the game with touchdowns; and the Pats won 45 to 7. Just before halftime, though, Brady threw a deep ball to Gronk and had it picked off by D'Qwell Jackson. As we now know, a Colts equipment manager tested that ball and found it a little flat. That report went up to the NFL game-day team and spawned a whole investigation that was never settled. To this day, the NFL staunchly holds that Tom Brady conspired with his equipment managers to let air out of the footballs that day. Brady and the Pats insist the frigid New England air was to blame.

The fight over deflated footballs would mostly be handled another day. Both Brady and Belichick held press conferences explaining their view of what happened with the balls, and then the Pats went to work preparing for the Super Bowl. Gronkowski was a major storyline going into the game. He won NFL comeback player of the year, which was hard to argue with after a dominant season following six surgeries. He also joined his rival Seattle Seahawks running back Marshawn Lynch on Conan O'Brien's late-night talk show to play a few hilarious rounds of the video game Mortal Combat.

The Super Bowl itself would not start great for Gronk, as he dropped a short pass right out of the gate. Thanks to that drop and two of the NFL's best defenses at work, the first quarter ended 0 to 0. The teams would trade scores in the second, when Gronk split out on the right side with only linebacker K.J. Wright guarding him. Almost everyone seemed to know the ball was going to Gronk. Brady lobbed it high, and Gronk caught it over his head in the end zone and never brought it down where it could get knocked loose.

The Patriots were in control, but then little-known Chris Matthews of the Seahawks, a guy who had been out of the NFL and selling sneakers at Foot Locker a few weeks before, came alive and the Seahawks scored a touchdown, field goal, and then another touchdown to go up 24 to 14. That run was aided by another pick thrown by Brady in the middle looking for Gronkowski. Patriots receivers Julian Edelman and Danny Amendola led the first 4th quarter drive for the Pats and the defense got a stop. Now Brady and company just needed a field goal to tie or a touchdown to go ahead. Tom Brady engineered a masterful drive that included two big passes to Gronk and a touchdown for Julian Edelman. The Seahawks now had 2:02 and needed a touchdown to win. Most football fans know what happened next. The Seahawks got down to the five-yard line, and they were running out of time. Marshawn Lynch ran four yards left and was stopped at the one-yard line. On second down, quarterback Russell Wilson opted for a short pass, and rookie defensive back Malcolm Butler jumped the pass and intercepted the ball with virtually no time left.

Rob Gronkowski and the Patriots were Super Bowl champs, kicking off an epic celebration. First, announcer Dan Patrick asked Gronk on the podium how it felt to be champs "again," momentarily forgetting it was Gronk's first win. Gronk was then the star of the victory parade, cruising through Boston chugging beers handed to him by fans. He appeared on *Jimmy Kimmel Live*, reading an excerpt from an erotic fan-fiction book called *A Gronking to Remember*. It was a good time to be Gronk.

Chapter 6: Rewriting the Record Books

The Patriots again entered 2015 with a fair amount of uncertainty. Tom Brady was a year older, and now facing a four-game suspension for football tampering that would be overturned temporarily right before the opening game. The Pats also lost their first round pick as a punishment. They said goodbye to Darrelle Revis and Brandon Browner, their top two defensive backs. Gronk had a healthy offseason, though, and was ready to go on opening day for the first time in awhile. The Pats also added Scott Chandler, another pass-catching tight end, to perhaps try and recreate the two-tight-end tandem that had been so successful with Hernandez.

Opening day brought a hard-fought battle against the Pittsburgh Steelers, one of the other top teams in the NFL. For one day at least, the "twin towers" were back. Gronk put up 94 yards and three touchdowns and Scott Chandler added a touchdown of his own. Gronk had another big game the next week against the Bills, putting up 113 yards and a touchdown. It was all needed, as the Pats won a surprising shootout 40 to 32. The Pats got comfortable for a few games after that. They crushed the hapless Jaguars, with Gronk putting up 101 yards, and then he put up 67 yards in a blowout of the Dallas Cowboys, who were cycling through backup quarterbacks with Tony Romo injured. The emotional rematch against the Colts went well, as Gronk scored a touchdown in a win. He added another touchdown and 108 yards in a close win against the Jets, and six catches and 113 yards in a win over Miami, including a short pass he grabbed midfield and took through a sea of defenders for a 47-yard touchdown. The Patriots beat down Washington the next week and then headed to the always-tough Giants.

Both defenses played well in the Pats vs. Giants matchup, but each made a huge mistake against the opposing superstar. Early on, safety Devin McCourty came up late to help on Giants superstar Odell Beckham Jr. and accidently took out Malcolm Butler, who was doing his best to keep up. OBJ took the ball 87 yards for a touchdown. The same thing happened to Gronk, as he caught a ball over the middle in the fourth quarter with defenders closing on him from either side, but he managed to slip out and the defenders knocked each other down, leaving Gronk to run 76 yards for a go-ahead touchdown. Gronk had another catch to help set up a last-second field goal, and the Patriots won by a point as time wound down.

The Pats followed up with a win the next week against Buffalo and were now 10 and 0, but the season was starting to take its toll. Scott Chandler and Danny Amendola were having trouble staying healthy, and running back Dion Lewis tore his ACL while receiver Julian Edelman broke a bone in his foot. The next game against Denver is where the fun really ended. Gronk scored early but got called for a crucial pass interference penalty in the fourth quarter. It was a problem that he was starting to have, as his physical style seemed to clash with a new emphasis by the referees on contact from both sides on passes. Then disaster struck late in the fourth quarter, as Gronk took a helmet to the knee and hit the ground hard. To many, it looked a lot like the hit in the Browns game that ended his 2012 season. To cap it all off, the Pats lost in overtime.

The Patriots were secretive about Gronk's injury, but the family released a statement saying he suffered a bone bruise and had no timetable for return. This again raised questions of whether the Pats and the Gronks were on the same page about his health situation. The Patriots would also lose the next game against the Eagles, as Gronk sat out and Brady struggled with the backup pass catchers available to him. Gronk returned the next week and put up a touchdown each week in wins against Houston and Tennessee. The Pats then lost their last two games, backing into the postseason with a record of just two wins and four losses in their last six games.

The slow finish did not hold back the Pats' offense in the first game of the postseason, against the Chiefs, who had demolished them the year before. Julian Edelman was back on a surgically repaired foot, and he paired up with Gronk to move the ball down the field to score a touchdown on the first drive. Gronk had a monster catch on a third and 13, grabbing the ball over the middle and then rumbling for 32 yards. He also had the touchdown catch, tying the all-time record for postseason TDs by a tight end. Gronk broke the record later in the game, putting the Patriots up 21 to 6 with a 16-yard touchdown grab. The Chiefs would come back to within a score, but the Patriots got the ball back and just needed one first down to end the game. Brady threw to Gronk, but the ball was tipped and bounced off Gronk and floated up into the air. Luckily, Julian Edelman was there to catch the loose ball, and the Pats won the game.

With that, the Patriots were onto their fifth AFC Championship Game, meaning Gronk had been on one of the last four teams standing every year after his rookie campaign. The challenger this year was the Denver Broncos, and the Patriots were favored because Peyton Manning was having a tough time putting any power into his throws, presumably owing to a previous neck injury. The Patriots struggled early, though. Gronkowski missed a pass on third down on the first two Patriots drives, and the Broncos built an early lead. The Patriots got a break when Manning threw a pass slightly backwards, making it a fumble that the Pats recovered and scored on, but Stephen Gostkowski, one of the best kickers in the league, missed the extra point. Brady later got picked off trying to go to Gronk and then missed him in the end zone on a key fourth down. Many would say Gronk was held on the play. After the game, he refused to say whether he was held, but he said he "couldn't even jump" and felt like his former teammate Aqib Talib "had me." Brady had also been pushed around all day by what many consider to be one of the best defenses assembled in the modern era. During the game, Gronk also had been spotted on the sidelines getting medical attention, and he would admit after the game that he was cramping up and was a little bit disappointed in himself for that.

Despite the struggles, late in the fourth quarter with the game on the line, Brady had one more chance and locked in on Rob Gronkowski. On fourth and 10, Brady lobbed the ball deep over Gronk's shoulder with two guys draped over him, and Gronk pulled it in for 40 yards. The drive would come down to another fourth down, this time on the four-yard line, and again Brady looked for Gronk, and Gronk delivered. Because of the earlier missed field goal, however, the Pats would need a two-point conversion to tie the game and send it to overtime. This time, Brady did not see Gronk, who many would say was wide open in the back of the end zone. Instead, Brady threw short to Julian Edelman and could not connect. Just like that, the season was over.

Chapter 7: Building a Legacy

Rob Gronkowski is no longer just a goofy young guy; he is now a veteran leader in the clubhouse. That presents Gronk with both challenges and opportunities. Gronk has stepped up as a face of the franchise while Brady scales back his media appearances. Because of Deflategate the Patriots lost a first-round pick, which hurt their draft class, and Scott Chandler had to leave football because of injuries. The Patriots did pick up Martellus Bennett, widely considered one of the top tight ends in the league, but he is coming off a couple down years. Many hope he will be the one to revive the two-tight-end combo.

Rob is working on cementing his legacy. He currently holds many single-season records based on his 2011 season: total touchdowns (18) and touchdown receptions (17) by a tight end in a season, as well as receiving yards by a tight end (1,327). That year, he was the first tight end to lead the NFL in receiving touchdowns. He has a record for most touchdowns of any player's first two seasons (28). He has the most multiple touchdown games in a season by a tight end (seven in 2012), and he was the youngest player with three touchdowns in both the regular season and the playoffs.

Gronk's current career marks are 405 catches, 6,095 yards, and 68 touchdowns. He is 27 years old, and looking back over the span of his career, the injury questions can be viewed in a different light. He has played five relatively healthy seasons in seven years and was the Pats' most reliable target in that stretch. His numbers are already approaching those of Tony Gonzalez, the current career leader in most tight end statistics, and he played 17 seasons. Gonzalez has 1,325 catches for 15,127 yards and 111 touchdowns. Gronk has already surpassed the touchdown totals for most other great tight ends, including Mike Ditka (43), Shannon Sharpe (62), and Kellen Winslow (45). Active tight end Antonio Gates has 111 touchdowns, but Gronk seems likely to challenge both Gates and Gonzalez for the career records. Gronk is tied for 42nd on the all-time receiving touchdowns list at any position, and matching Jerry Rice's record of 197 touchdowns does not seem out of the question.

Despite Gronk's prolific media profile, he has kept his love life largely under wraps. That changed a little bit in 2016 as former Patriots cheerleader Camille Kostek confirmed the two were dating. If Gronk ever decides to build a family of his own, he should be financially secure. He has said repeatedly that he has never spent a dime of his NFL contract money, instead living off his endorsements and other earnings. For example, in the 2016 offseason, the Gronkowski family set up a private cruise and charged people for the opportunity to spend a few days on a board with the brothers. He has been creative about making money. For one other example, he is known to travel around with his family in a limo bus, so he sold the rights to a company in Buffalo to build a fleet of 25 matching busses to rent out to the public as Gronk Busses. It has also been reported that he is negotiating for a new contract, as his one-time record-setting contract has now been surpassed by far less talented players.

It seems certain that the NFL will be blessed with many more incredible plays and hilarious antics by the one and only Rob Gronkowski.

About the Author

Benjamin Southerland is a lifelong Chicagoland resident. Southerland developed a strong interest for politics and government during his college years through his study of leaders who have shaped history, such as Winston Churchill, Napoleon, and Thomas Jefferson. Southerland is also interested in individuals who have impacted the world of sports and entertainment. He has studied and written about politicians, world leaders, athletes, and celebrities. He researches these fascinating figures extensively in order to determine what has shaped their worldviews and contributed to their success. He aims for his books to give readers a deep understanding of the achievements, inspirations, and goals of the world's most influential individuals. Follow Benjamin Southerland at his website benjaminsoutherland.com to learn about his latest books.

Made in the USA
Lexington, KY
14 December 2017